Granny Root

grows fruit

KANEPRESS

AN IMPRINT OF ASTRA BOOKS FOR YOUNG READERS

New York

follow
my food

For Jenny and Karin—*DC*

For Jonathan and Louise—*JG*

First published in the United States in 2024 by Kane Press,
an imprint of Astra Books for Young Readers, a division of Astra Publishing House
astrapublishinghouse.com
Printed in China

Originally published in Great Britain in 2021
by Scallywag Press, London

Library of Congress Cataloging-in-Publication Data

Names: Chancellor, Deborah, author. | Groves, Julia, illustrator.
Title: Granny root grows fruit / by Deborah Chancellor ; illustrated by
Julia Groves.
Description: First edition. | New York : Kane Press, 2024. | Series: Follow my food |
Summary: "A child narrator helps her Granny grow fruit through the year, as they put in new plants in
the fall, prune in the winter, weed and hang nets in the spring, and water and harvest in the summer.
Backmatter includes a matching game, more information about growing fruit, types of fruit,
and a kid-friendly recipe"— Provided by publisher.
Identifiers: LCCN 2023025164 (print) | LCCN 2023025165 (ebook) | ISBN
9781662670701 (hardcover) | ISBN 9781662670695 (ebk)
Subjects: LCSH: Fruit-culture—Juvenile literature.
Classification: LCC SB357.2 .C43 2024 (print) | LCC SB357.2 (ebook) | DDC
634—dc23/eng/20230717
LC record available at https://lccn.loc.gov/2023025164
LC ebook record available at https://lccn.loc.gov/2023025165

First American edition, 2024

10 9 8 7 6 5 4 3 2 1

Design by Ness Wood.
The text is set in Foundry Sans Medium.
The title is hand lettered.
The illustrations are created in cut paper and digital media.

Granny Root
grows fruit

by Deborah Chancellor
illustrated by Julia Groves

KANE PRESS
New York

Granny Root is busy in her garden.
She works all year to grow fantastic fruit.

Fall brings strong winds and storms. I help to rake up piles of fallen leaves,

while Granny spreads the soil
with steamy compost.

Granny digs holes in the ground for some new raspberry plants. Together, we plant a blueberry bush.

Winter comes with icy frost and snow.

Granny cuts back
tangled apple branches
and prunes her
favorite pear tree.

Spring breezes in with sun and showers.
Granny plants some strawberry seedlings.

We dig up weeds, to give the tiny seedlings space to grow.

The strawberry plants
begin to blossom.

We hang nets over the flowers, to stop birds from pecking the fruit that will form.

Summer sunshine dries the earth.

Granny waters . . . and waters . . . and waters . . .
to save her crops from wilting in the heat.

Granny checks her fruit to see if it is ripe.

Her crops are ready to pick at different times.

We don't want to harvest the fruit too soon,
or leave it too late!

The apples and pears are
ripe when summer ends.

I collect all the windfalls
in my basket, but I
can't resist a sweet
and crunchy bite!

Granny Root's fruit
is so tasty and fresh.
We eat what we can,
and then bake
or make jam with
the rest.

Follow the trail of seeds to match the words and pictures.

Fruit is ripe when it is ready to pick and eat.

A weed is a wild plant that grows where it is not wanted.

When you harvest a crop, you gather it in when it is ripe.

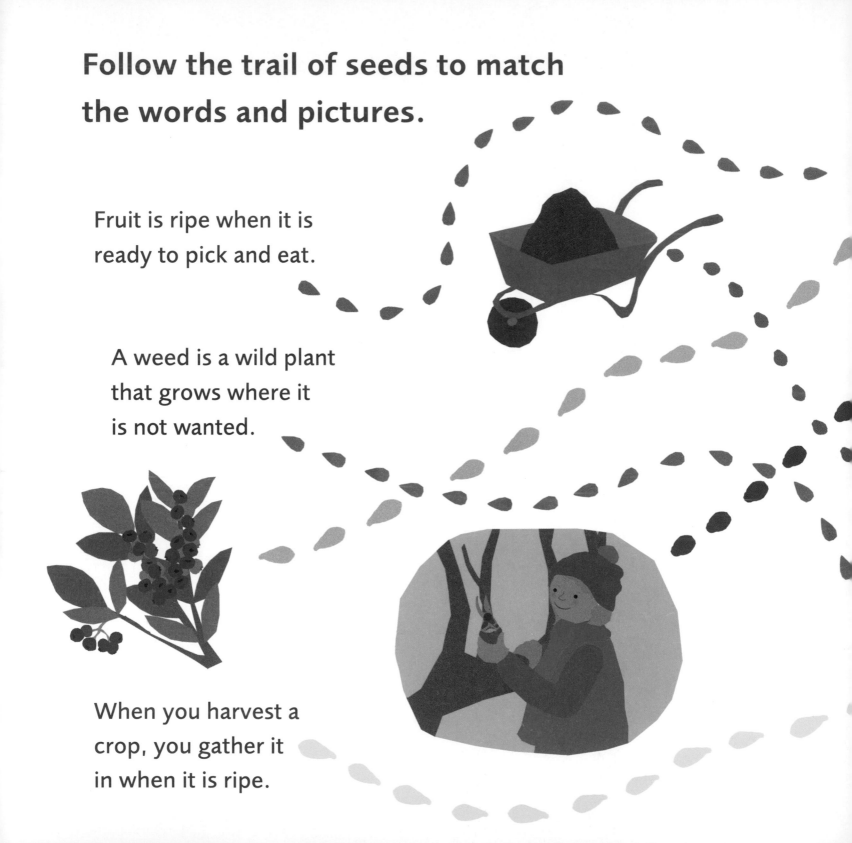

Crops are plants that are grown to be gathered and eaten.

When you prune a plant, you cut off unwanted branches, so it grows better next year.

Compost is natural waste that is used to feed soil and help crops grow.

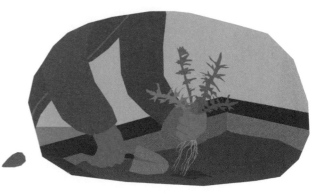

Plants need water

All plants need food and water to survive. They use water to carry food up to their leaves and back down to their roots. Water is precious, so use it wisely—don't waste tap water on plants. Instead, collect water in a water barrel, to sprinkle on your fruit and vegetables when the ground around them is dry.

Close to home

Fruit is grown all over the world. Some of it travels many thousands of miles to end up in your lunch box! This uses lots of fuel, which is bad for the planet. You can help by eating fruit that was grown closer to where you live. That means only eating local fruit at certain times of the year, when it is ripe and ready to pick.

Sweet sun

Some kinds of fruit plants love the sun. Their leaves soak up energy from the sunshine. The sweeter fruit tastes, the more sun it needs to grow. Strawberries are very sweet, so it's best to plant them in sunny spots. Blueberries and raspberries have a sharper, tart taste, so they can put up with some shade.

Different fruit

It's fun to grow your own fruit. Ask a grown-up to help you plant some seeds. Here are some dierent kinds of fruit.

Berries

avocado

blueberry

Stone fruit

cherry

peach

Pome fruit

apple   pear

Dry fruit

hazelnut   walnut

Make a fruit salad

The vitamins and minerals in fruit
help you to stay healthy.
Eat fruit every day if you can!
Ask a grown-up to help you make this tasty fruit salad.

You will need:

2 red apples	8 strawberries
3 plums	2 bananas
2 oranges	2 pears

12 seedless grapes
(Or use other kinds of fruit.)
2 tablespoons of honey
1 glass of apple juice

Instructions:

 1. Peel the oranges and split
them into segments.

2. Cut the orange segments, plums,
grapes, and strawberries in half.

3. Slice the apples, pears, and bananas.

4. Put all the fruit in a bowl.

5. Mix the honey with the juice and pour
over the fruit. Stir well and eat.

Do your part

Growing fruit and vegetables uses up fewer natural resources than raising animals. You can help the planet by eating less meat. Instead, eat nutritious plants that are grown locally.

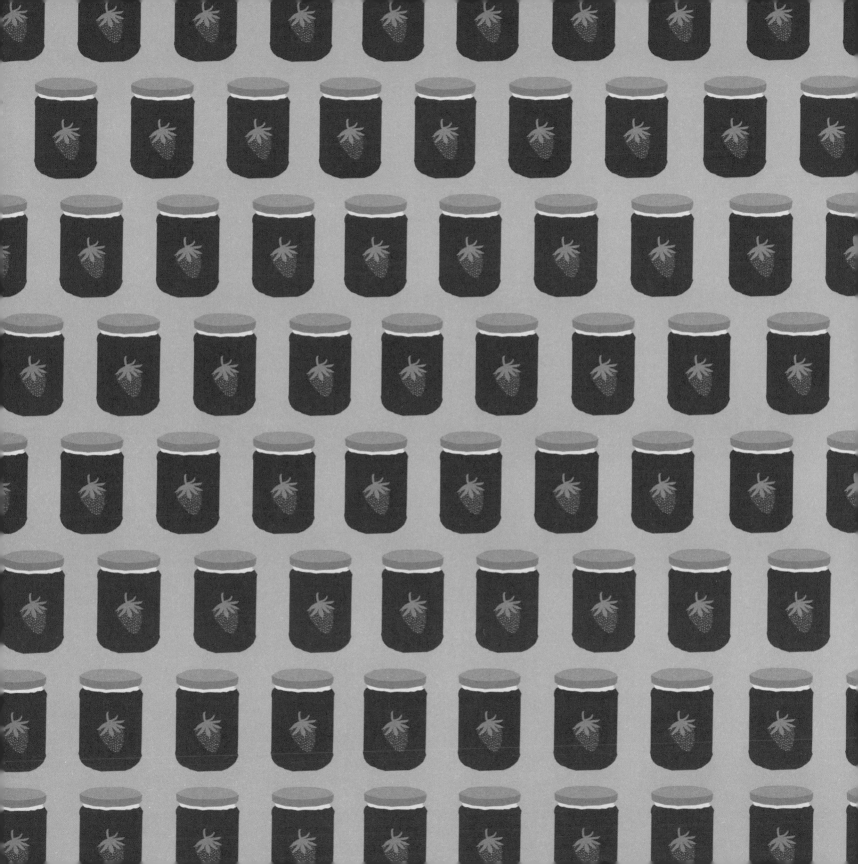

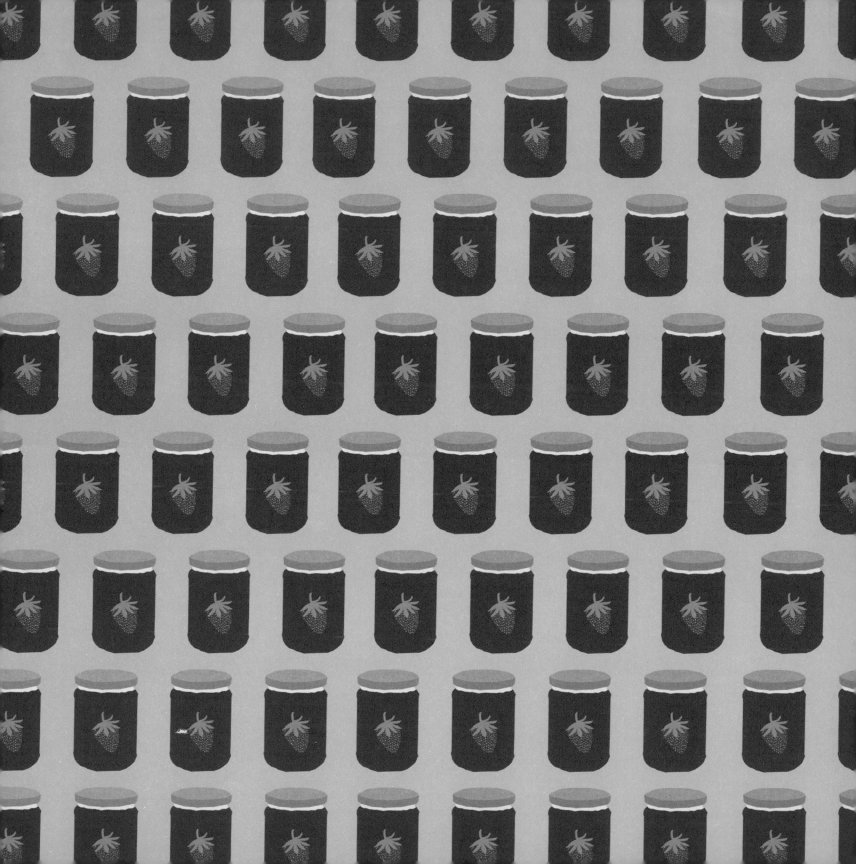